BEDFORDSHIRE

A PICTORIAL GUIDE BY
ERIC MEADOWS

based on the original text by SIMON LARKMAN

DUNSTABLE PRIORY CHURCH

1975

WHITE CRESCENT PRESS LTD
LUTON

Copyright 1975
White Crescent Press Ltd
ISBN 0 900804 10 6

In this third edition the original text by Simon Larkman has been fully revised, with a new Introduction, by Eric G. Meadows, who also supplied the photographic illustrations.

Printed and Published by
WHITE CRESCENT PRESS LTD, LUTON, ENGLAND

CONTENTS

ILLUSTRATIONS NOT IN GAZETTEER

ABBREVIATIONS USED

App.   = Appendix
c.   = circa or about (c.1760)
C   = century (18C)
N., S., E. & W. = north, south, east and west
(q.v.)   = which see

Architectural styles (see App. 2):
Trans.-Norman = Transitional-Norman
E.Eng.   = Early English Gothic
Dec.   = Decorated Gothic
Perp.   = Perpendicular Gothic

STATISTICS

Latitude	51°48' to 52°20' North
Longitude	0°8' to 0°41' West
Overall length	36¾ miles
Overall breadth	22¾ miles
Area	476 square miles (305,056 acres)
Highest Point	801 feet (Dunstable Downs)
Lowest Point	50 feet (Little Barford)
Average Rainfall	22 inches to 28 inches (highest among downs)
Parliamentary Divisions ..	5 – Bedford, Luton East and West, Mid-Beds and South Beds

Population – County   ..

1801 Official Census   63,000
1861 Official Census 135,000
1931 Official Census 221,000
1951 Official Census 312,000
1971 Official Census 464,000
1974 Official Report 483,000

– Administrative Districts 1974:

Bedford	129,000
Mid-Beds	95,000
South-Beds	94,000
Luton	165,000

– main towns 1974:   ..

Ampthill	6,000
Bedford	74,000
Biggleswade	10,000
Dunstable	32,000
Flitwick	5,200
Houghton Regis	12,000
Kempston	14,000
Leighton Linslade	23,000
Luton	165,000
Sandy	6,000
Stotfold	7,000

(70 per cent of the population is in these towns)

INTRODUCTION

Bedfordshire, probably the smallest county in England, may seem very ordinary to the average person travelling on any of the seven major routes through it from London to the north – Watling Street (A5), the M1 Motorway that has relieved the A5, the A6 through Luton and Bedford, the Great North Road (A1) and three railways. It probably seems rather flat, a succession of fields of corn or cabbages relieved by urban sprawl, marred by accretions of pylons, with gaping pits and smoke-belching chimneys of brick and cement works. All these are there but much more besides for anyone who will look closer and search out its charms.

As in most areas, what you will see – its landscape, buildings and ultimately how its people live – are determined by geography, weather and geology, especially the latter. Fortunately Bedfordshire has great variety in its geology – in the south chalk hills, part of the Chilterns, rise 300–450 feet above the undulating gault vale a few miles wide; then the Lower Greensand Ridge extends across, west to east, in a band one to five miles wide (their largest exposure north of the Thames); to the north of which is an Oxford Clay plain over which the Great Ouse meanders; finally in the north-west are low hills of oolitic limestone. Also most of the area is blanketed with glacial deposits of boulder-clay and gravels.

The landscape, decided by what lies beneath it, is often pleasant though not spectacular. The downs are sometimes sheep-grazing or for recreational use, with beechwood plantings. They grow hawthorn and elder scrub where not grazed, but rich flora including pasque flowers, rockroses, knapweeds, harebells and many varieties of wild orchid among their grasses. Often cornfields come to the very edges of their steep slopes. Cornfields and some pastures on the gault with decreasing hedge-rows, but a few elms, oaks and ashes remain. The Greensand has more estates with parkland, cattle rearing and forested areas, but market-gardens on the light soils that give early crops of vegetables. A little flower-growing near Potton and more vegetables on glacial sands and gravels in the north-east. Mixed farming in the north-west with more trees and some hedges retained.

Building materials followed the geology in the past: flint had to be used in the south, also a harder bed at the bottom of the Lower Chalk was extracted by tunnelling at Totternhoe Knolls, hence called Totternhoe stone. It was used alone or with flint for houses and churches, ideal

BARTON HILLS

WILD LANDSCAPES

FELMERSHAM Nature Reserve

for interior carving but it weathered badly outside. The Greensand, golden-brown in colour, contains iron and has occasional boulders of a coarse rusty sandstone (called ironstone) which was used for building locally. In the north-west the limestone, dug up as small irregular lumps, was used in the Ouse villages and towards the Northamptonshire border. Also the river was a transport route for some better stone to be brought in from Northamptonshire, which allowed spires to be built. Everywhere the heavy soils grew oak as well as elm; there was plenty of straw and some reeds for thatching.

The people's occupations were controlled and are still affected by the land. Farming was the main livelihood and is still an important one, while market-gardens are in the valleys of the rivers Flitt and Ivel. The heavy lands with sufficient rain and warm summers are ideal for corn. The straw, plaited for hat-making, gave Dunstable and Luton their former basic industry. Today most corn is for brewing and for biscuit-flour. From the clay, tiles were made in the late 13th century at Dunstable; brickmaking started about two centuries later and has developed with the railways and new processes into a major industry in mid-county. Cement is made at Sundon and, until recently at Houghton Regis, but chalk from quarries at Kensworth and Totternhoe is now sent as slurry by pipeline 54 miles to Rugby Cement Works. Sand is excavated from the Greensand, especially near Leighton Linslade, and gravels by the Ouse near Harrold, Radwell and Blunham.

Now let us consider the landscape in more detail – its typical and better parts. The downlands, by common consent the finest scenery, mount to just over 800 feet on Dunstable Downs with wide views to west, north and east. The London Gliding Club is sited at their foot to use the rising air currents they create, so no wonder that this open breezy spot, partly owned by the National Trust, is popular. Further downland to the west is preserved in Whipsnade Zoo. An outlier of these downs is Totternhoe Knolls, of Lower Chalk now heavily quarried for cement manufacture, leaving the summit above the village, topped by motte and bailey earthworks, as a nature reserve for chalk flora with views in every direction. Scenery that is more lovely is in the stretch of lower downs from Sundon to the Barton Hills, with Deacon Hill farther east beyond the wooded intrusion of Hertfordshire at Hexton. Much of this escarpment is broken by coombes with wooded sides, leaving tongues or spurs between them; hence The Clappers south-east of Sharpenhoe, where the largest northern Clapper crowned by a beechwood is owned by the National Trust. These hills face northward over more wooded farmland to the Greensand Ridge, countryside marred only by a lime-works below Barton Cutting, estate housing in Barton and the drastic reduction of hedgerows. South of the church at Barton is a small valley with the Springs beyond arable fields, a beech-hanger on its west edge

SHARPENHOE and The Clappers from Sundon Hill

DOWNLAND

SHARPENHOE and cornfields from The Clappers, looking to the Green-sand Ridge beyond Samshill

and its eastern side a delightful group of grassy humps and hollows, grazed by sheep and cattle.

There are views to the downs from low hills in the gault vale at Billington, Stanbridge, Toddington, Harlington, Pulloxhill and Shillington; also bordering the Greensand at Gravenhurst, Meppershall and Dunton. On the south edge of the Greensand is Flitwick Moor, a bit of primaeval marshland where water has led to peat formation. It is now a Trust nature reserve as it is perhaps the best location in the county for general natural history.

The Greensand Ridge has more woods throughout its length with heather, gorse and bracken flourishing on sand outcrops like Sandy Warren, a Trust nature reserve which includes the Royal Society for Protection of Birds' headquarters. There are magnificent parks and forested heaths at Woburn – the ducal domains – at Ampthill, at Southill, Old Warden and Ickwell; also at Hassells near Sandy. Good viewpoints are northwards from Aspley Heath, Ridgmont and Lidlington; also in both directions at Ampthill Park, but brickworks are included in the last three. More fascinating are the glimpses and little views that keep appearing as one travels. Near Biggleswade and Potton the country is lower and open, often featureless like Cambridgeshire which it borders.

ON THE GAULT

Cornfields near Hanscombe End, SHILLINGTON, where poplars add a French quality.

Utcoate Grange, WOBURN

GENIAL COUNTRY OF THE GREENSAND

Looking W. over HUSBORNE CRAWLEY

In Stockgrove Country Park near HEATH AND REACH (see App. 4)

Incidentally the brickworks at Stewartby have given one asset to the ravaged landscape of the Oxford Clay vale – a flooded pit is used for sailing, supports a large colony of Black-headed Gulls and is visited by other waterfowl.

The Ouse valley has some beautiful stretches, especially at Biddenham where a few old once-pollarded willows grow and by Bromham Park. Farther upstream the valley is narrower between slightly higher hills, its best reach – tranquil water in lush pastures with enough oaks and willows – from Felmersham (with nature reserve) up to Harrold and on to Turvey, where the river's west bank is the county boundary.

Most true old Bedfordshire is the quiet hilly district north of Bedford, without railways or main roads. The only recent intrusion is the aerodrome built in wartime west of Thurleigh, which has modern wind-tunnel buildings of the Royal Aeronautics Establishment at its south end, but being on the hill's edge above Milton Ernest they are seen more from the Ouse valley. Otherwise the rather poor soils of this still lonely land are well-farmed, more arable than pasture but with many bits of woodland, remnants of the forest that was large in mediaeval times. The villages are small without housing estates, except perhaps for Riseley and Thurleigh. Brick and timber with a plaster rendering, often colour-washed, were used for the older houses; usually little buildings with thatched or tiled roofs, and red pantiles for weather-boarded outbuildings.

Looking to the bridge at BROMHAM

THE GREAT OUSE

From the bridge at FELMERSHAM

The buildings of the county include very few that are architecturally outstanding, Felmersham having perhaps its best church. The better buildings, mostly churches, include in different periods: *Saxon* – part of towers at Clapham and Stevington; *Norman* – Dunstable, Elstow and Kensworth; *Early English* – Chalgrave, Eaton Bray, Felmersham and Studham; *Decorated* – Dean, Langford, Lower Gravenhurst, Luton, Shillington, Sundon, Swineshead, Wymington and Yelden; *Perpendicular* – Bedford (St. Paul's), Colmworth, Flitton (of ironstone), Leighton, Luton, Marston Moretaine, Odell, Toddington, Totternhoe, Willington, Someries Castle (Hyde) brickwork, *c.*1470; *Tudor* – Hulcote (or Holcot) church 1590. Elstow Moot Hall *c.*1500, Old Warden Gostwick building on Abbey site with *c.*1540 brickwork, Willington manorial buildings; *Jacobean* – Houghton House ruins, Meppershall manorhouse; *Renaissance/Georgian* – Ampthill Park and Avenue House in Ampthill, Aspley House at Aspley Guise, Bedford *Swan Hotel* and Harpur School, Eggington House, Hinwick House and Hinwick Hall, Moggerhanger Park, Wrest House 1834–36 and Archer Pavilion at Wrest 1709–11 in Silsoe, Southill, Woburn Abbey; *Victorian* – Ridgmont and Woburn churches, Milton Ernest Hall, 'Cottage orné' and House at Old Warden; *Recent* – Ampthill Courthouse, Bedford County Hall, Felmersham housing in Trinity Close, Pavenham housing in Plaiters Close, Whipsnade Zoo elephant house.

How long man has been here we can only conjecture from evidence of archaeologists. Palaeolithic land surfaces were discovered in the faces of brickmakers' claypits at Luton, Caddington, Kensworth and Whipsnade by the Dunstable historian Worthington G. Smith, who found a flint-working place at Caddington and linked chips with flint tools after perhaps 250,000 years – a record of his patience and skill. Mesolithic flint arrowheads have been found in gravel at Leighton Linslade and on hills at Sandy (where three Iron Age forts are). Neolithic man had a trading site at Maiden Bower, Dunstable and lived at Waulud's Bank, Luton. He, with Bronze Age man left barrows – the best Chiltern burial-mounds – at Five Knolls on Dunstable Downs and a few on Galley Hill. Iron Age man also lived at Maiden Bower, on Sharpenhoe Clapper and at Ravensburgh Castle by the county boundary above Hexton, Herts. Dray's Ditches north of Luton were Bronze and Iron Age boundaries. All these sites are near the very ancient route, Icknield Way, on the forest-free chalky land.

Lynchets or banks formed in tillage of the chalk escarpments – the land in our area least disturbed by man – probably date from the Bronze Age to Saxon times, when most flatter or lower ground was forest or swamp. The lynchets are a monument to labours of unknown men.

The Romans may have had a posting station where their Watling Street crossed Icknield Way. Certainly a few Romans lived and farmed

STUDHAM: Stiff-leaf and scalloped capitals of Totternhoe stone, c.1215

13C CRAFTSMANSHIP

TURVEY:
Ironwork on S. doors,
c.1270

thereabouts; likewise at Sandy, probably a little Roman crossroads settlement.

During the next six centuries Saxons and Angles came, probably by the rivers Lea and Ouse; later West Saxons moved in along the Chilterns (Icknield Way). A lot settled here and gave us many of our present village names – hoo, hou- (Houghton), -soe (Silsoe) from 'hoh' meaning hill (Clophill or Odell); -'ton' meaning a farm (Sutton or South Farm) or down corrupted to 'ton' (Toddington) or 'don' (Sundon), 'ham' meaning home (Clapham), cot (Hulcote), -ey or islet (Sandy, Turvey), Totternhoe and Warden mean watch hill – to give just a few examples. Danes came from 835 and made earthworks for their settlements as at Water End, Renhold. Fifty years later Danelaw (Danish land) and Wessex by a treaty of King Alfred were bounded here by the river Lea, a line to Bedford and the river Ouse to Watling Street. The only record of a battle in our area was in 917 when the Danes attacked Bedford, then a Saxon king's town.

From the Norman Conquest, history has no major events to record here. Man continued to till the soil and, with increasing population, to clear more forest and drain marshes. There were markets at Ampthill, Bedford, Biggleswade, Dunstable ('Hill Market' of Houghton manor), Harrold, Leighton, Luton, Potton, Shefford, Toddington and Woburn; of which Dunstable and Shefford were trading centres without farmland. Demand for skills grew in every way and craftsmen increased; some working together in a group or guild, such as the stonemasons who shaped and carved Totternhoe stone into stiff-leaf capitals as at the churches of Chalgrave, Eaton Bray, Elstow, Luton and Studham 1210–40, again about 1340 for the baptistry and tower at Luton – all work of great artistic merit. Likewise, in the mid or later 13th century, a guild of blacksmiths including Thomas of Leighton (who made the grille for Queen Eleanor's tomb at Westminster Abbey in 1293) made ornamental hinges for church doors at Eaton Bray, Leighton and Turvey. For about three centuries there were two rural industries not connected with farming – pillow-lace making introduced in late Tudor times and, a little later, rush-mat making in riverside villages.

Our little county has yielded few nationally great people. John Dunstable (c.1375–1435) was an early composer of music, John Tiptoft of Everton turned 'Butcher of England' and Margaret Beaufort, born at Bletsoe, became ancestress of English kings. Our greatest son, John Bunyan of Elstow, the 'Immortal Dreamer', writer and preacher changed religion in England. Later, Admiral Byng lived at Southill and John Howard of Cardington strove for prison reform. Besides these we have a few writers – poet George Gascoigne of Cardington and Thomas Norton of Sharpenhoe, together pioneers of secular drama; Elkanah Settle of Dunstable rivalled Dryden; Dorothy Osborne of

At FELMERSHAM, looking N. to Sharnbrook spire

THE OUSE VALLEY

At BLETSOE, looking N.W. to Sharnbrook spire beyond the railway viaduct

Chicksands and poet Nicholas Rowe of Little Barford. Craftsmen there are too such as Thomas Tompion, son of the Ickwell blacksmith, who became one of the first watchmakers and Joseph Paxton of Milton Bryan, designer of the Crystal Palace.

Population figures reflect the state of our farming county in historic times. In 1086 the population was very small – estimated about 1,000 for Bedford and 700 each for Leighton and Luton. In 1801 the county had 63,393 people with nearly 4,000 in Bedford. By this time the markets of Ampthill, Harrold, Potton (after a fire in 1783), Shefford, Toddington and Woburn were small or dwindling; these places had populations of 1–2,000. Slightly larger were Leighton on the canal and Luton on the St. Albans to Bedford road, both with populations about 2,800. Biggleswade (following a fire in 1785) and Dunstable grew rapidly from increased road-traffic. A fast increase in population at this time caused much poverty on the land, so migration to towns or emigration. Towns grew quickly, especially with the coming of railways – Leighton 1838, Bedford branch to Bletchley 1846, Dunstable 1848 and Luton 1858, the Midland Railway via Sharnbrook, Bedford and Shefford to Hitchin in 1857, and from Bedford through Luton in 1868, lastly the Bedford to Northampton branch in 1872. Because of the railway Sandy became a market-gardening town, Ampthill and Leighton grew slowly, while Dunstable without coaches remained steady. However Bedford, because of the excellence of its schools, grew steadily – even rapidly in the 1880s – so in the sixty years 1831 to 1891 it increased fourfold to 28,023; Luton in the same period increased $7\frac{1}{2}$ times to 30,053, due to its flourishing hat industry. The 1891 population of the county was 160,621.

In the first half of this century changes began. The chief one was establishment of engineering and manufacturing industries using electricity in Bedford, Dunstable and Luton; industries affected little by the inter-war industrial depressions, so many people moved in from depressed regions. Dunstable's population quadrupled to 17,109, Luton's threefold to 110,381 but Bedford's barely doubled to 53,075, the county's total in 1951 being 311,937 (about doubled). Brickmaking developed into a giant industry, with cement manufacture and sand extraction on a large scale. For nearly twenty years airships were built and flown from Cardington, where two giant hangars are still a landmark. Henlow is a long-established R.A.F. Station, by Cranfield airfield is the Cranfield Institute of Technology, Thurleigh has a Royal Aeronautics Establishment and Luton opened a civil airport in 1938. In the country farming revived after years of depression, but market-gardening increased steadily especially with road transport. Many mansions were taken over by institutions, such as Wrest at Silsoe by the Institute of Agricultural Engineering and Ampthill Park as a Cheshire Home (with the park as a public one for the town).

STEWARTBY: Claypit and brickworks

INDUSTRIES
Biggleswade and Leighton Linslade are developing factory-estates

LUTON: Part of Vauxhall Motors Ltd. works

In the last twenty-five years greater and more fundamental changes have taken place than ever before, due to the internal combustion engine. The motor car has allowed townspeople to live farther from their workplace; also to live with a view of fields is highly prized. As a result our villages have become settlements of commuters, with spaces infilled and estates added of monotonous urban dwellings. Often much of the original village, or at least its High Street, has been demolished to widen the main road; often traffic noise has become worse in a village than a town side-street. Larger villages in many cases have become festers of urban sprawl. The countryside too is changing. In our county farming is still a major industry but with the horse replaced by the tractor, with combine-harvesters, silos and changed methods, farming employs far fewer people. With mechanisation for arable crops, hedges are not wanted so are hacked down or torn out; also isolated trees become fewer – loss to the landscape is far greater than the economic gain. Excavation of chalk, clay, gravel and sand scar the land. Local government planners now control use of land and all kinds of development, so the worst excesses are avoided but pressures are great. Statutory authorities too can be among the vandals. Reinstatement of waste land is now more usual; other wild parts are nature reserves, habitats for plants, birds and insects much diminished by intensive farming.

Despite all the changes and pressures on it, Bedfordshire still has much to offer the interested searcher – gentle countryside, natural and man-made beauty impregnated with history. It is hoped that more of its delights will be found in the following pages.

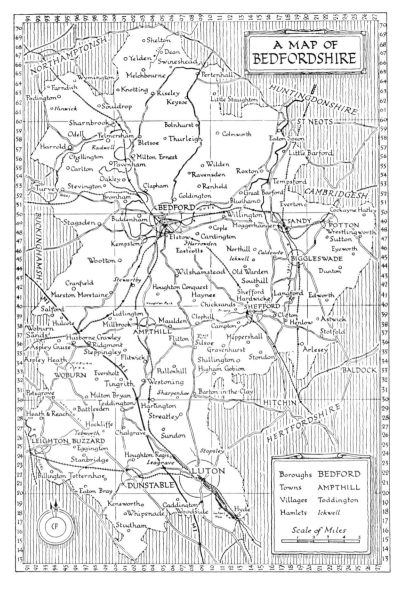

A MAP OF
BEDFORDSHIRE

Boroughs	BEDFORD
Towns	AMPTHILL
Villages	Toddington
Hamlets	*Ickwell*

Scale of Miles

NOTE: Since this map was drawn, minor boundary changes in 1965 have added Linslade and excluded Eaton Socon.

GAZETTEER

The figures after each place-name are National Grid map references.
Bedfordshire is covered by Sheets 153, 165 and 166 of the 1:50,000
Series O.S.
(Sheets 113, 134, 146 and 147 of the discontinued One-Inch Series O.S.)

AMPTHILL: Church Street with Avenue House 1780, its doorway and larger extension by Holland 1792–95 (see App. 4)

AMPTHILL (0338), created the royal honour by Henry VIII in 1542, lies on the Greensand Ridge in fair countryside. It has a variety of beautiful old buildings, many of them 17–18C and some Tudor. *The White Hart*, a former coaching inn, was built in the days of Queen Anne and incorporates a Tudor building. Opposite is a Georgian arcaded shop. 28 Church Street, a mid-Georgian house, has the wrought iron gateway and screen from Houghton House (see Houghton Conquest). Facing Church Close is Dyvenor House of 1725, Georgian Brandreth House and the little whitened Feoffee Almshouses.

The ironstone church, on the edge of open hill-country, has Dec. arcades and chancel arch; otherwise is Perp. with carved angels under the roof, but over-restored externally. Four brasses include one to William Hicchecok, a 'wolman' 1450 and to Sir Nicholas Harvey 1532 who attended Queen Katherine; also there is an impressive monument to Richard Nicolls, whose family lived at Ampthill Park in the 17C. Nicolls took over New Amsterdam from the Dutch in 1664 and renamed it New York after his patron the Duke of York, but at the Battle of Solway Bay in 1672 a Dutch cannonball killed him. The ball is in his monument, 'instrumentum mortis et immortalitatis'.

Henry VIII was a frequent visitor to Ampthill Castle, and it was there that Katherine of Aragon lived from 1531 until divorced in 1533, when she was moved to Kimbolton. The site of the castle is in the park, marked by a cross erected by Lord Ossory in 1770, with an inscription by Horace Walpole on its base, commemorating 'the mournful refuge of an injured Queen'. The castle was built in the 15C by Sir John Cornwall, later Lord Fanhope, from ransoms after the Battle of Agincourt.

The present house in the park was built 1686–88 for the Dowager Countess of Ailesbury and Elgin, by architect-mason Robert Grumbold of Cambridge. It was sold to the first Lord Ashburnham in 1690, altered by John Lumley 1705–07 when the N. front was made; lastly side wings and redecoration, including elaborate ceilings, were added

AMPTHILL PARK: N. front, with doorcase and decoration by Chambers

1769–71 by Chambers. In 1818 it became the home of the famous Lady Holland (died 1845), whose gatherings at Holland House, Kensington, were the most brilliant of her day. The house is now a Cheshire Home, and the park is a public one with some grand trees including a few old oaks.

On the W. edge of the town near Littlepark Farm is the Oxford Hospital, an almshouse of 1697 in Wren style, of chequered brickwork with original windows, dormers and a single-handed clock on a central pediment below a cupola – a little gem, backed by Scots pines in a rural setting.

ARLESEY (1936). Mentioned in the Domesday Book as a market town, Arlesey extends for two miles along the road following the little river Hiz, and suffers for its elongation in a certain lack of character. At the S. end a considerable brick and tile industry is sited by the railway; also the vast psychiatric Fairfield (Three Counties') Hospital between Arlesey and Stotfold (q.v.).

The church is largely Dec. with some E.Eng. work in the chancel, where the E. window has Dec. flowing tracery. Perp. is the tall rood screen and the mutilated E. Anglian font carved with Crucifixion and Garden of Eden. Unique in the county is an Elizabethan family pew with thin columns and a broad frieze of dolphins. The W. tower is of 1877.

Between the river Hiz and the railway to S. of a new bridge over the railway by the former station is a Trust nature reserve for aquatic plants, which contains the moat originally round the manorhouse.

N.E. of the railway station is Etonbury, 9C earthworks of a Danish raiding centre near the meeting of the rivers Hiz and Ivel.

ASPLEY GUISE (9435), meaning 'Aspen-clearing' of the family of Guise who first held the manor here in late 13C, lies among the woods and sandy hills typical of this part of the county, and is noted for its evergreens – particularly holly hedges.

Beautiful Aspley House, built c.1690, is attributed to Christopher Wren – perhaps his sketch design with a perfect E. front beyond cedars; its W. face early Georgian (see App. 4). Near it, Guise House is early Georgian and off a byroad is Old House of Elizabethan timber and brick.

The church, originally Perp., has been considerably altered. There is an effigy of Sir Wm. de Tyrington c.1400, also brasses to a priest kneeling beside St. John Baptist c.1410 and to a Guise – probably Sir John of 1501.

Around the tiny market place with central shelter, individual buildings cluster harmoniously. Pleasant little Victorian houses, many in pale brick, can be found in S. streets.

ASPLEY HEATH on a wooded hillside

Farther W. beyond Aspley Wood is the small village of Aspley Heath, on a hillside, with good houses – large and small – Victorian church, convalescent homes and a view to N. In the church are Clutton's single columns and original rose-window with a cross, 1868. By the main road is Henry VII Lodge, an 1811 attempt at a perfect Tudor house.

ASTWICK (2138) is a tiny and charming village containing practically no houses, but two old farmhouses – Church and Bury with a moat – a 1720 red-brick Old Rectory and a mill by the Ivel. The small church is Perp., with an earlier mediaeval tower having a large blocked arch on its S. side – a puzzle – but formerly it may have opened sideways into an earlier nave.

BARFORD, GREAT (1352) lies by the river Ouse, which is here crossed by a stone bridge of seventeen arches which dates from 15C, widened in the 19C with bold Victorian brickwork giving character. It is a pleasant village without being in any way remarkable, but has modern development. College Farmhouse in High Street is three-storeyed red-brick Georgian with a pedimented doorway; also smaller 17C and 18C houses remain.

The church has a pinnacled Perp. tower, a Saxon nave with long-and-short E. quoins, but its aisles are Victorian. The glazed tower-screen with large geometric tracery – the most impressive feature here – is early 19C. In the chancel is a small brass to a man and wife c.1525, also a monument to Thomas Anscell 1591.

William Foster is buried in the chancel. He was related by marriage to Francis Wingate of Harlington (q.v.) who committed John Bunyan to prison after his arrest at Lower Samshill (see Westoning). Bunyan records that Foster tried to persuade him to give up preaching, apparently by some show of affection. For this the tinker labelled him 'Judas', and popular opinion holds that he is the original of Mr By-Ends in *The Pilgrim's Progress*. He afterwards became a magistrate and a man of influence in the county, earning lasting unpopularity through his bigoted interpretation of the laws against Nonconformity.

GREAT BARFORD: Bridge Farm, church, 'The Anchor' and part of the brick-faced bridge

BARFORD, LITTLE (1857). A memorial stone in a cottage garden marks the birthplace in 1674 of Nicholas Rowe, who became Poet Laureate under George I and was buried in Westminster Abbey in 1718.

Little Barford is a very small village; beyond it, the cubes and towers of the Power Station 1945–47. In fields by the Ouse and Victorian manor-house, its redundant church has two Norman windows, Norman S.

doorway, part of an old screen and a brass to Thomas Perys with his wife, 1535.

BARTON-IN-THE-CLAY (0831). Because of the widened main road through it, a big housing estate and a lot of modern housing, Barton has ceased to be one of the county's more charming villages. The only picturesque part is near the foot of the hills, especially around the church, where 17C and 18C cottage-rows are now one house in orchard gardens. The Rectory is partly Elizabethan. Rectory Farm E. of the church, trees and the playing-field keep this corner rural. However the Willes' manorhouse stands, end-on to Manor Road, Faldo is an old moated house; there are a few thatched cottages and pleasing houses. On the W. edge is a little weather-boarded watermill, *c.*1790.

The church has a Perp. W. tower of nicely varied materials. Inside are E.Eng. arcades – massive piers contrasting with slender columns and stiff-leaf of the responds – a good Dec. (but restored) roof with angels and carvings supported on corbels with faces; also linenfold pews. The E.Eng. chancel has Easter sepulchre, piscina, three sedilia and some mediaeval floor tiles. On the wall are brasses to Philip de Lee 1349 and Richard Brey 1396.

The beautiful Barton Hills are popularly supposed to be the original of Bunyan's 'Delectable Mountains'.

BARTON HILLS: 'Plum Pudden' from Barton Springs valley

BATTLESDEN (9628) is a very small nostalgic place off Watling Street. The church, of no great interest itself, contains a monument to Sir Saunders Duncombe who introduced sedan-chairs to England in 1634.

Sir Joseph Paxton (see Milton Bryan) worked as a youth in the park and, in 1821, made the lake. The house was pulled down in 1885 and the park given over to farming, but an avenue and view to Dunstable Downs remain.

BEDFORD (0550) strategically sited where a minor Roman road crossed the Ouse when the river was the main highway, the infant town had its castle and later a minster-church. It was occupied successively by Saxons and Danes. Edward the Elder re-occupied the town during the re-conquest of the Danelaw and made a settlement on the S. bank protected by the King's Ditch, still traceable. In 917 his men repulsed the Danes' attack and from Bedford they sallied forth a few months later to massacre them at Tempsford (q.v.). In 1009–10 more strife, when Danes came down the Ouse 'to Bedford, ever burning as they went'.

The Norman barony of Bedford was in the hands of the Beauchamps, one of the three major baronies in the shire at the time of the Domesday Survey. The Beauchamp castle stood N.E. of the old bridge and was the scene of numerous encounters, the last being in 1224 when Henry III ousted Falk de Bréauté, King John's favourite, and restored the site to William de Beauchamp (from whom Falk had taken it), first having destroyed its fortifications (see Beauchamp, App. 3). Nothing of the castle now remains except the mound.

Bedford's subsequent history is peaceful. It was neutral during the Civil War and, although it was occupied in turn by both Royalists and Roundheads, there was no serious shedding of blood. The county gaol, in which Bunyan (see Elstow) was imprisoned, stood at what is now the High Street corner of Silver Street, marked by an inscription on the pavement.

Of the mediaeval town very little remains except four notable churches, of which St. Paul's is the chief and largest. Originally there was a Saxon church on the site, followed by a Norman building which was pulled down by Falk de Bréauté to strengthen the castle walls. The present church is partly Dec. and Perp., over-restored in the 19C when the tower, spire and transepts were added. It is a 'hall' with its clerestory above the aisle windows; this gives a spacious interior. Perp. are fine roofs in nave and S. aisle, carved misericords in the chancel, a traceried screen in S. aisle and a stone pulpit skilfully adapted from a reredos, from which John Wesley is said to have preached his famous 'Great Assize' sermon in 1758. There is a brass to Sir William Harpur 1573, also the matrix of the earliest known English brass – that would be to Simon

Beauchamp 1208 (see Goldington). F. C. Eden improved the interior, especially the chancel.

St. Peter's chancel was a late Saxon nave, and the now central tower has a Saxon base, with Norman belfry-openings and 19C top. Victorian too is the present nave, but the S. doorway is a fine Norman one from St. Peter Dunstable formerly opposite St. Mary's.

In St. Mary's S. transept, small late Saxon windows have been found, but Norman are its N. transept and central tower having large belfry openings. The interior is whitewashed plaster, the N. arcade Perp., otherwise much restored.

St. John's has a Dec. chancel containing sedilia, piscina and priest's door. This chancel was the chapel of St. John's Hospital founded by Robert de Parys. To the chancel was added the aisleless nave (much restored) and the Perp. W. tower. A former building of the hospital, just N. of the church, looks early Victorian-Tudor, but is restored inside to show the timbered roof and stone walls of the mediaeval refectory.

A Tudor building is hidden behind the 1756 stone front of the old Harpur School (now mayoral suite). This Free School was endowed by Sir William Harpur, whose statue is on the front. Two Queen Anne houses of red brick stand near St. Mary's, and Crofton House in St. Cuthbert Street is early Georgian – best of the few survivals of the little country town.

BEDFORD: 'The Swan' Hotel on The Embankment

About 1800 Bedford began to grow. The Duke had the river made navigable by barges, which increased trade. He also had *The Swan* built by Holland in 1794, 'the noblest English hotel of the age, very severe and classical with its ashlar masonry and pediment' (Pevsner). The staircase of 1688 from Houghton House was fitted into it. Nearby, the stone bridge was rebuilt 1811–13 to a graceful design by Wing (widened in 1923) – a magnificent centrepiece. Numbers of boys at the school increased enormously and genteel families came to the town, building charming Regency houses as at the start of Kimbolton and Bromham Roads, in The Crescent and Adelaide Square.

BEDFORD: Bridge from S.E., with 1880 Shire Hall and St. Paul's spire

Sir William Harpur born at Bedford in 1496, a merchant-tailor in London and its Lord Mayor in 1561, endowed Bedford School in 1566 with 13 acres of fields in Holborn. This bequest increased so enormously in value that the Harpur Trust was set up to administer it. Now there are four schools. The best buildings are the free Tudor-style Girls High by Champneys 1882, but Dame Alice uses a Regency house of stone. Blore's 1830–38 façade for the Modern now screens a new shopping centre from Harpur Street. After a big fire the Trust built forty-six Tudor-style dormered houses of brick in ranges 1801–06, later made into almshouses, now in Dame Alice Street.

Bedford has long been a stronghold of Nonconformists and there are numerous chapels in the town. Most interesting is the Bunyan Meeting House 1850 standing in Mill Street, on the site of 'Ruffhead Barn' in which Bunyan preached. It contains many relics of the inspired tinker, including his anvil, chair, iron fiddle, his will and many translations of *The Pilgrim's Progress* (see App. 4). The very fine bronze doors, presented by the Duke of Bedford in 1876, are the work of Frederick Thrupp; their ten panels illustrate scenes from *The Pilgrim's Progress*. The Howard Chapel 1849 (founded by John Howard and others in 1772) is also in Mill Street. Near it, Howard House, built for use on his frequent visits from Cardington.

BEDFORD: Bronze of John Bunyan, with plaques of 'The Pilgrim's Progress'

The Victorians gave the town some great assets – the impressive Embankment, riverside gardens among willows with a suspension foot-bridge, a second roadbridge (cast iron), the red-brick Shire Hall by Waterhouse 1880, a life-size bronze of Bunyan by Sir Edgar Boehm on St. Peter's Green and of Howard by Sir Alfred Gilbert on an Art

Nouveau plinth in St. Paul's Square and, to the north, a park with lake and variety of trees. They also brought railways, rows of rather mean housing, and engineering works.

The last twenty years have seen sweeping changes, good and degrading. A well-planned Bus Station and new shops in All Hallows, but heartless tower flats nearby. Tower blocks of the Mander College and new Town Hall contrast well with the older riverside buildings, but the latter is too big and unsympathetic to St. Paul's Square. The extensive County Hall, its bulk lightened by the design and white finish,

BEDFORD: County Hall 1968–69, with part of Mander College beyond Prebend Street Bridge 1883–84

uses the waterfront excellently, but the crude concrete slab of *County Hotel* brutally rends its lovely setting. Nearly as bad is the Granada tower in St. John's Street. A necessary third roadbridge and relief road have been carved out; they should leave some of the centre quieter and more pleasant.

The town, now with cosmopolitan residents, has expanded northwards as large well-planned estates. Here is the only hill, Manton Heights (on which are new buildings of Bedford Modern School), which gives perhaps the best general view of Bedford (see App. 4).

C

BIDDENHAM (0250), near as it lies to Bedford, has not suffered the fate of its neighbour Clapham (q.v.), as it is off the main road. For nearly a century prosperous Bedford people have built good houses here; among them remain some thatched cottages and the stone, half-timbered *Three Tuns*. The village is now much enlarged.

BIDDENHAM from Box End, Kempston, over riverside pastures

The church, in its lovely wooded churchyard near the Ouse, is mainly Dec. and Perp., though the chancel arch is Norman. The late-Perp. N. aisle windows are finely detailed. There is a brass to three members of the Faldo family *c.*1490, and two early 16C brasses of unknown women in shrouds; also a mural monument to William Boteler 1601 and his wife (see App. 3). In the tower is a Flemish tapestry 1549, signed 'Rolof Vos'; its history is unknown. The traceried screen in S. aisle should be seen.

In 1857 a deep shaft here was found to contain Roman sculpture, pottery and a skeleton. Four years later James Wyatt made most important discoveries of Old Stone Age implements in river gravels, together with remains of extinct prehistoric animals.

BIGGLESWADE: High Street

BIGGLESWADE (1944) in the fertile Ivel valley, is still a centre of thriving market-gardening, of milling, agricultural engineering and manufacturing industries. Its market place, visually unrewarding (like most of the town), the common to the N., and coaching inns recall its past. In 1785 a fire destroyed 103 houses, but the Great North Road brought trade then.

Of its individual buildings, the former Town Hall 1844, with two giant columns, is outstanding. Near it, the former Market House and *White Hart* are Tudor but much restored. *The Crown* is mid-Georgian.

Its large church is mainly Perp. – grand vaulted S. porch, good roof to S. aisle and a chancel rebuilt in 1467 by John Ruding, to whom there is a very badly damaged brass, 1481. There is also a broken brass to William Halstead 1449 and his wife. The tower was rebuilt in 1720.

BILLINGTON (9422) is a small village on a low hill in the gault, looking W. and N. on the Ouzel valley and S. to the Chilterns. The little Victorian church with bell-turret has an E.Eng. blank window inside. Manor Farm is 17C.

BLETSOE (0258). This quiet attractive village, set in the gently rolling country of north Bedfordshire, was the birthplace of 'The Mother of the Tudor Dynasty', Margaret Beaufort.

The manor of Bletsoe passed from the Beauchamps to the St. Johns at the end of the 14C, when Margaret Beauchamp married Sir Oliver St. John (see App. 3). On his death she married John Beaufort, Duke of Somerset, of which marriage Margaret Beaufort was born in 1443. She married Edmund Tudor and became the mother of Henry VII. Margaret had three husbands and finally separated from the third, Lord Stanley, leading an almost nun-like existence until she died in 1509.

Of the Elizabethan mansion, which superseded Bletsoe Castle where Margaret was born, one wing now remains, incorporated in a farm-house. Inevitably it is claimed that Queen Elizabeth visited this mansion, so did James I.

The Dec. church is much restored. In a barrel-vaulted chapel are monuments to the St. John family, the finest being that to Sir John St. John 1559, who kneels with his wife and nine children. He was a relative of Henry VIII, with whom he was brought up under the care of Margaret Beaufort. In the church too is a 15C wall painting of St. George and the Dragon; also an interesting modern stained glass window on the 400th anniversary of the printed Bible.

The *Falcon* on the main road was famous in coaching days and Edward Fitzgerald, translator of *Omar Khayyam*, stayed there.

BLUNHAM (1551). This small but growing village, near the junction of the Ivel and the Ouse, still has a cluster of old houses in its centre. A roughcast gabled one opposite the church was the 16C manorhouse. Thatched buildings include the old school, near which is a Baptist chapel of 1751.

Blunham House, a plain building, was the home of Sir Peter Payne, an early 19C reformer considered dangerously 'advanced' because he advocated education for women. He also agitated for repeal of the Corn Laws and was opposed to slavery, although a large part of his fortune was derived from the West Indies.

The church, of mixed styles mostly Perp., has an imposing W. tower, late Norman with a Perp. top and W. window as late as 1583. The chancel has well carved roof-bosses. There is a Dec. canopied tomb in the chancel, a brass to Richard Maulaye 1506 and an alabaster tomb of Lady Susan Longueville, the Earl of Kent's niece who died in the manor-house in 1620. A rector from 1621–31, while Dean of St. Paul's Cathedral, was the poet Dr John Donne.

BOLNHURST (0859), meaning Bolla's Wood, tells of former woods of which there are remnants; also several moats show old sites of homes. Now the pleasing village by the Kimbolton road adds to the weekly devotions of its inhabitants the pleasure (or penance) of a Sunday walk, for the church is alone half a mile towards Thurleigh. The Perp. and restored building has a big W. tower of good proportions. Inside is a mediaeval wall painting of St. Christopher and a memorial to a Master of Chancery, Sir John Franklin 1707, which records (could it be with mild surprise?) that although large sums of money were entrusted to his keeping, he never used them to his own advantage.

The half-timbered and colour-washed *Plough* is probably Tudor.

BROMHAM Bridge, looking to the Mill (right)

BROMHAM (0051), now a very large village, has retained some of its rural charm – thatched cottages, orchard trees and a green; also it is off the main road. It stands W. of the Ouse, which is crossed by a 26-arch bridge and causeway, the arches over the main channel dating from the 13C. The mill on the W. bank bears the date 1695. It is a chilling reflection for the summer visitor that, in 1281, a woman was carried from this bridge to Bedford on an ice-floe!

Bromham Hall, up-river, was the home of Sir Lewis Dyve (1599–1669), Bedfordshire's most ardent Royalist in the Civil War. In the park stands the church, alone on a rise overlooking the river. It is mostly Perp., with a N. arcade *c.*1300; its chancel with Dyve Chapel by Butterfield, 1868. It contains a notable brass to Thomas Wideville 1435 and his two wives, the monument of which Sir John Dyve 1535 appropriated to himself and his mother; also a wall-monument 1732 to Lord Trevor, the first Chief Justice to be made a peer.

CADDINGTON (0619), set high on the downs, is a large village with a green, housing estates and new dwellings, but it has very ancient associations. Towards the end of last century Worthington G. Smith, the noted Dunstable archaeologist, made a discovery of great significance. By careful study of flint tools found in the neighbourhood, he eventually tracked down a flint working-place of the Old Stone Age, 250,000 years old. He found flint tools made here, also flakes struck off in shaping them; he actually fitted some of these flakes on the stones from which they had been chipped!

The church has a late Norman S. doorway, and the W. wall of the nave has quoins that may be Saxon. A Dec. E. window (into the present vestry) is an oculus and the best feature. The Perp. W. tower has a nice mixture of stone, flint and brick.

The poet Cowper received his early education here and Thomas Pickford, founder of the firm of carriers, lived at Mayfield Farm. The parish includes the village of Woodside, with a church of 1890, and hamlets of Aley Green, Slip End (slype or field-strip) and Pepperstock on the county boundary, all unprepossessing except for some flint-walled houses in Woodside.

CALDECOTE (1645), formerly a hamlet of Northill, is concerned with market-gardening. Its church by Blomfield 1867–68 is of yellow brick with red brick bands.

CAMPTON (1338), a growing village on the Greensand, is the burial place of the poet Robert Bloomfield, (1766–1823). His tombstone bears simply the dates of his birth and death with the words: 'Let his wild native wood-notes tell the rest'. He was born in Suffolk, son of a tailor. At first he worked on the land – an occupation ill-suited to his frail constitution – so he was apprenticed to a shoemaker. For many years he lived in abject poverty in London, but the publication of his most famous poem, *The Farmer's Boy*, brought him literary distinction and financial independence. He lost his money in an unsuccessful business venture and retired to Shefford (q.v.), where he died.

The church has an E.Eng. S. doorway and S. arcade, Dec. chancel and late-Perp. N. arcade, but has been partly rebuilt and much restored. It contains a Dec. screen under the tower, tiny brasses 1489 and, in a late-Perp. chapel, monuments of 1655 to the Osbornes of Chicksands (q.v.).

Opposite the church is an Elizabethan manorhouse in which, in 1645, Sir Charles Ventris was shot at through a window by one of Cromwell's men. A bullet-scarred panel remains as a memorial to their bad marksmanship. Nearby, the imposing red-brick front – mid-Georgian – of the Old Rectory hides an older house.

CARDINGTON (0847). This small, neatly-kept village, with trees and a little green by its church, owes much to its most esteemable residents, John Howard and his close friend and second cousin Samuel Whitbread. The Whitbread family (see App. 3) lived in the charming red-brick early Georgian house opposite the church. Samuel was apprenticed to brewing in 1734 and after his business success bought most of Cardington, where many houses have 'S. W.' on them. Howard built estate cottages by the green 1763–64. Of these men, diarist John Byng wrote: 'They strive which shall most benefit and adorn it'.

CARDINGTON: estate houses by part of the green

John Howard, born in London in 1726, came to a Cardington farmer when his mother died. Years later, about 1756, having been a war prisoner of the French, he lived at the handsome Georgian house which stands N. of the church (see App. 4). In 1773 he was appointed High Sheriff, responsible for the county gaol. He saw its awful state, with the gaoler dependent on ex-prisoners' fees; so in that year began his tour of prisons over England and across the Continent. Unlike so many re-formers, he enjoyed immediate official sympathy and, in 1774, was passed the first of a number of Acts to improve the lot of prisoners. From Cardington he set out on his last tour, to be struck down by fever and buried in a Russian village in 1790. Perhaps it is not unnatural that his own wishes of burial were ignored: 'Give me no monument, but lay me quietly in the earth; place a sundial over my grave and let me be forgotten'. His burial at Kherson was attended by great crowds; there is a memorial statue, by John Bacon, in St. Paul's Cathedral and another in Bedford. So long as prisons remain part of our judicial system John Howard will never be forgotten.

Except for the late-Perp. chancel and S. doorways, the church was rebuilt – a brutal act – in 1898–1902. It contains one of the richest collections of monuments in the county. Two splendid altar-tombs have brasses to Gascoigne 1540 and Harvye 1638 in armour, two busts to Ive Whitbread by Scheemakers *c*.1768, Samuel Whitbread 1796 by John Bacon with large white relief, and Samuel Whitbread 1849 by Weekes with kneeling figures. A rarity here is a black font, 1783 by Josiah Wedgwood (1730–95); the only other such font is at Essendon, Herts. The 20C is represented by the impressive eagle lectern.

At Cardington Cross, half a mile towards Bedford, there is a cross frequently described erroneously as an Eleanor Cross. It was erected in 1796 and restored by Chantrey in 1837. Nearby is a small and dignified five-arched bridge built in 1778 by John Smeaton (1724–92), engineer of the Eddystone Lighthouse.

In the now demolished Elizabethan manorhouse (Manor Farm) probably lived the poet, soldier and M.P., George Gascoigne (died 1577).

The great hangars which housed the R.101 and her sister airship still jut into the sky at the nearby R.A.F. station. Victims of the crash in 1930 are buried in a mass grave, with dignified monument by Sir Albert Richardson, just inside the gates of the cemetery. Recently a small experimental airship has been tested here for economic weight-carrying and low-speed uses.

CARLTON (9555), the Danish 'Carla's Place', was a small village, enlarged recently by new housing. Its High Street retains some stone houses; two of them tall, thatched and end-on to the street so probably 17C.

The church dates back to the Normans, of whose work some fragments remain – a blocked N. window in the chancel and the font. There is a charming little Perp. screen. In the chancel floor is the tombstone of Thomas Wells who was the incumbent for 70 years and died in 1642, 'aged above a hundred'. A brass tablet commemorates Joane Goddard, who – to the delight of the village punsters – went Godward in 1610. The diarist, Benjamin Rogers, was rector 1720–71.

An approved school for boys was established half a mile S. of the village in 1857 – one of the first in England and now a Community Home.

CARLTON: High Street

CHALGRAVE (0127). Thought to be a considerable village at one time, Chalgrave now has only a farm by its church among horse-chestnuts, with a fair view to the Chilterns. It is not clear what caused its inhabitants to desert their village. Tebworth (q.v.) and Wingfield are large and developing hamlets in this parish, the latter especially with nondescript housing.

The top of the church tower fell during a storm in 1889 – failure of the Totternhoe stone as at Eaton Bray. Its interior is delightfully unrestored, with the floor now below ground-level. Consecrated in 1219, it has its original N. arcade with very fine leaf-carved capitals, but Dec. the S. arcade, with character in faces on corbels, and the chancel which has a lovely piscina. In the 1930s, hidden under the inevitable whitewash, were discovered extensive wall paintings of 1300 to 1460 (most of 1300). There are two effigies of 14C knights, one of which is supposed to be of Sir Nigel Loring (died 1385–86), hero of Conan Doyle's books *The White Company* and *Sir Nigel*, although his arms do not appear among those on the tombs. The Lorings were lords of the manor.

Dr Dodd, a vicar of Chalgrave, was hanged at Tyburn in 1777 for forgery. He was also rector of Hockliffe.

CHALTON see **TODDINGTON**

CHELLINGTON (9555), an unremarkable village adjoining Carlton, has its church half a mile away set on a hill in the middle of a field, with nothing but a grassy track to connect it with the road. From it there are fine views over the Ouse and surrounding countryside. The church is of mixed styles, originating in E.Eng., with Dec. W. tower and spire.

CHICKSANDS PRIORY: E. front by Wyatt 1813, with 15C oriel

CHICKSANDS (1239). Roeisa, wife of Payne de Beauchamp (see App. 3), founded Chicksands Priory in 1150, in the Gilbertine Order – the only monastic order originating in this country. It was for both monks and nuns; also not a learned order, books and study being discouraged. The priory's history is unsensational.

The priory church has long since gone, but preserved are a fine E.Eng. doorway, a vaulted undercroft and part of the Perp. cloisters among the further domestic buildings, with massive roof-timbers, incorporated in the present house. They are the only remains of domestic buildings of this order. The house, remodelled by James Wyatt in 1813, is now part of a large R.A.F. base, so the house is not open to the public. The base has erected a vast radar antenna – a new landmark – on the Greensand Ridge.

Chicksands Priory is known chiefly as the home of Dorothy Osborne (1627–95), whose family came into possession of the priory in 1576 (see App. 3). At twenty-one Dorothy fell in love with William Temple, but the match was opposed by her family, largely on political grounds. She had many other admirers including Henry Cromwell, Oliver's son, but she remained steadfast to William, writing him a series of letters about her everyday life at Chicksands which are some of the most interesting in the English language. In true fairy-tale tradition, she did eventually marry her 'prince' and enjoyed a long and happy married life; but, sad to record, her beauty was permanently disfigured by small-pox before her wedding day.

CLAPHAM Church with tall Saxon tower (Norman top)

CLAPHAM (0352), a large main-road village, can be forgiven its many ugly modern buildings for its church preserving a fine Saxon tower, probably 10C. The tall tower was originally defensive, and entry was only by a triangular-headed doorway 20 feet up. The present ground-level doorway and arch leading into the nave are Norman, as is the bell-stage. The church was largely rebuilt in 1861 by Sir G. G. Scott, but the chancel arch is Norman and the arcade mainly E.Eng. The monument to Thomas Taylor 1689 has an inscription worth reading.

CLIFTON (1638), meaning 'Cliff Farm' above the Flitt, is a large village with a lot of modern housing, but keeps a few pleasant parts. Its church has a Dec. nave and chancel, with a Perp. W. tower and grand N. arcade; all extensively restored in 1862 when the impressive N. aisle was rebuilt by Edward Haycock. There is an elaborate alabaster monument with effigies, to Sir Michael Fisher 1549 and his wife; by it, a brass to their son, John Fisher 1528.

CLIFTON: The village pond is now a garden

CLOPHILL (0837) extends along the N. side of the little Flitt valley, between sandy hills covered with woods. The main road (A6) crosses the valley and its dual stretch uphill to the N. is most lovely, among sweet-chestnuts and pines; well-planned too, with birches and gorse on the central divide.

The village, E. of the main road, starts with the old *Flying Horse*, a wee green with limes and nearby a brick lock-up; then a long street of varied buildings. They include Georgian red-brick Clophill House, behind wrought-iron railings with stone urns on piers and parapet; opposite is Ivy House and a former mill.

The church of 1848 by T. Smith of Hertford, like his Silsoe one, seems convincingly mediaeval. It has an Elizabethan screen from the old church on the hill, now a ruin though its Perp. W. tower is nearly intact.

At Cainhoe, to the S.E., are earthworks of the Norman motte and bailey castle of Nigel d'Albini (see App. 3).

CLOPHILL: *Cainhoe Castle motte and Chicksands antenna*

COCKAYNE HATLEY (2649) takes its name from the Cockayne family (see App. 3) who held the manor from early 15C to 1745, when it passed to the Custs. It is a tiny and fair village, the most easterly in the county.

Its church, away in open fields, has a pinnacled Perp. W. tower and a E.Eng. N. arcade. It was fitted with fine Baroque wood-carving by the Rev. H. C. Cust, rector 1806–61. The choir-stalls with backs dated 1689 and very Catholic, are from the Abbey of Aulne near Charleroi, the altar-rails from Malines, the tower screen from Louvain and N. aisle screen from Ghent. Good mediaeval glass from a Yorkshire church is in the finely detailed Perp. E. window of the N. aisle. There are four brasses to Cockaynes, 1430–1527, and a mural monument to Sir Patrick Home 1627.

The poet W. E. Henley is buried in the churchyard. Henley was a friend of Sir James Barrie, and it is said that his baby daughter's pronunciation of 'friend' suggested to Barrie the name 'Wendy' in his story of Peter Pan.

COLMWORTH (1158), a fair but straggling village, well-endowed with trees, has a lovely church, prominent with its lofty spire. Near it are Manor Farm, partly 17C, and a tree-girt Georgian rectory.

This noble church is without aisles, so its windows are large. It was entirely rebuilt, perhaps by the Braybrooks, and has the harmony given by a single style – Perp. with its spaciousness and fine proportions. The Dyer family's alabaster monument of 1641 is excellent.

Timothy Matthews, a great evangelist of the 19C, is buried in the churchyard, brought here from Bedford where he died of typhus in 1845. He held a curacy at Colmworth for some years, travelled extensively and collected vast crowds by blasts on a trumpet.

COPLE (1048), set in the rather flat land to S.E. of Bedford, is an attractive village. By the main road is a tollgate cottage, a few Bedford estate houses and some thatch remain among newer housing. 17C much-gabled houses face the church and, hidden by trees, Cople House is Georgian but derelict.

The Perp. church, with earlier W. tower, has a 15C traceried screen. It contains a number of good brasses – Nicholas and Pernel Roland, also Walter Roland, both c.1400, John and Margaret Launceleyn 1435, Bulkeley family 1556 (unusual design) and early 16C Thomas Grey family. Also in the chancel, a brass to Sir Walter Luke 1544 and his wife, Anne who was nurse to Henry VIII. Sir Walter was granted the privilege of wearing his hat in the king's presence – a fact illustrated on a shield bearing the word 'ley' (law) and a hat on a corbel.

Samuel Butler, author of *Hudibras*, lived here for a few years in the service of Sir Samuel Luke of Wood End, a noted Parliamentary leader during the Civil War.

COTTON END – see **EASTCOTTS**

CRANFIELD (9542) has become a very large village, due largely to brickmaking in the area and to Cranfield Institute of Technology with its airfield. However it is undistinguished, though it has some Victorian almshouses. Its church has Norman work in its blocked doorway, E.Eng. arcades and Perp. the roofs with carved bosses.

There are several theories as to the origin of the former industry of lace-making in Bedfordshire. An interesting one is that a party of Flemish lace-makers from the Mechlin country settled at Cranfield in 1588, as a result of religious persecution in their own country. Lace-making was general in the northern part of Bedfordshire and in the neighbouring counties of Buckingham and Northampton.

DEAN (0467), divided into Upper and Lower, an unspoilt village sited in twisting leafy lanes of the remote N. of the county. Dean House

Farm is partly early-Tudor and has Jacobean panelling. Larger but plain Dean House is late Georgian and gabled Lodge Farm is 17C. Towards Shelton, the 1850 tower windmill has become a stark ruin.

The church, mostly Dec., has a short spire on its W. tower which has extra fine bell-openings, quaint gargoyles and one hand on its diamond clockface. The perfect rural interior has been preserved intact – E.Eng. chancel arch and barred N. doorway, Dec. the unusual S. doorway with original door and both arcades (heightened for Perp. clerestory). Perp. are all the very good roofs – carved with angels and open frieze over the nave – also the pews, three remarkable screens and the font with large roses on its base. A brass is to Thomas Parker, a priest, 1501 and there is a quaint almsbox. Above the pre-Reformation pulpit is the Dillingham family's memorial tablet.

Francis Dillingham born here (see Wilden), was translator of the Book of Isaiah for the Authorised Version of the Bible.

DUNSTABLE (0122). The history of this place begins on the Downs, where there is a group of Neolithic and Bronze Age barrows, in each of which was probably a central burial. In the 1920s the most northerly one was excavated by Sir Mortimer Wheeler and yielded interesting relics including a polished flint knife by the Neolithic woman's skeleton.

The road from the Downs into Dunstable (Tring Road) follows roughly the line of the Icknield Way, and to Totternhoe Knolls runs the Green Way, possibly equally ancient. Hereabouts, when the Romans occupied England in 1C they found a few British people. The Romans built Watling Street and, near to the crossing a mile to the E., perhaps had a small posting-station.

Saxons passed this way and later lived here (relics found in Marina Drive are in Luton Museum – see App. 4). The first real settlement was in early 12C, when Henry I had woods cleared and built himself a house (Kingsbury), encouraging his subjects to settle about him on this part of his manor of Houghton already known as Dunestaple ('dune' – hill and 'staple' – a market) – a trading place with little farmland. The town was big enough c.1115 for the Norman schoolmaster Geoffrey of Gorham to teach and to produce a miracle play.

In 1132 the king founded the Augustinian Priory S. of Kingsbury. During the following centuries the town was the scene of numerous tournaments, an important synod was held there in 1214 and, in 1533, the Priory housed the court which pronounced its judgement of divorce against Katherine of Aragon (see Ampthill). Henry I, Stephen, John, Henry III, Edward I, Edward III, Henry VI, Henry VIII, Elizabeth and Victoria is the impressive list of royalty who have visited the town. The body of Queen Eleanor, on its way to Westminster, rested for a night before the altar of the Priory church in 1290. An Eleanor Cross stood in the market place, until it was destroyed by Essex's soldiers in 1643.

John Dunstable (died 1453) was probably a native. Very little is known of his early life or of his career. He was something of a mathematician, but is known for his music – for the mass and motets. There is no doubt too that his work was famed on the Continent, but the school of composers which he led in England was obliterated in the Wars of the Roses.

In 1648 Elkanah Settle, Dryden's close rival, was born at an inn here, son of a 'barber chirurgeon'. From literary greatness he was reduced to impoverished obscurity and died in the Charterhouse in 1724.

For a century from 1742, coaches passed through the town, reaching a peak of eighty a day. *The Sugar Loaf* dated 1717 and the Georgian *Saracen's Head* were coaching inns; part of the older *Anchor* is an early 17C pillared gateway. Priory House (Council offices) has elegant early Georgian fronts, and has preserved a vaulted mediaeval room of the Priory. The former Chew School 1719 bears a curious turret cupola, also a handsome doorway with figures of two charity boys on it; adjoining, the plain 1723 Cart Almshouses. All these buildings are in High Street N. and S. In Church Street, *Old Palace Lodge* (Hotel) on the site of Kingsbury has, to its east, the 1745 Marshe Almshouses, with a quietly dignified white front.

DUNSTABLE Priory Church S. aisle, with Norman piers (c.1150) and vaulting (replaced 1865 except two E. bays)

As at Elstow, all that remains of the magnificent Priory church is the Norman nave of seven bays, because it was used as the parish church. The great portal is Norman, the remainder of the W. front E.Eng. with a much ornamented N.W. doorway, but Perp. are the N. aisle and restored tower. Inside, the restored Norman vault of the S. aisle is very competent; it has increased the monastic atmosphere of this building which keeps the best Norman work in the county, originally about twice as long. There are notable memorials, several brasses and the famous Fayrey pall, gift of Henry Fayrey 1516, a merchant, and of the Fraternity of St. John the Baptist whose portraits are embroidered on the red brocaded cloth.

DUNSTABLE: Queensway Hall 1962–64

During Victoria's reign the town grew slowly, its main industry the making of straw hats. Then, as Luton expanded to its boundaries, more industry and people came to Dunstable – Vauxhall and Chrysler motor factories, printing works and many others. The population has risen from 5,000 to 32,000 in the past seventy-five years, with widespread housing estates which meet those of Luton. This has necessitated a new traffic-free shopping area and a new civic centre with domed Queensway Hall, Library and offices. Of the same date and designers as the hall is a circular brick Catholic church 1962–64 in West Street. The Victorian town is disappearing rapidly, its character seen best in West Street.

The town is noted for its beautiful Downs, rising to 800 feet with glorious views across two counties. On fine weekends crowds gather to enjoy the air and watch the activities of the London Gliding Club, whose flying field is at the foot of the downs – here modern man soars above ancient (and new!) earthworks.

DUNSTABLE Downs, looking N., with a glider

DUNTON (2344), a sizeable village set on a ridge, is visible from a considerable distance. The large church is Dec. and Perp., but restored at Victorian rebuilding of the tower. It contains graceful Dec. windows especially the grand E. one, a Dec. sedilia and a Georgian organ.

Flowers are grown on market-gardens here.

EASTCOTTS (0845). A civil parish including Harrowden (q.v.) and Cotton End which has a good Tudor brick manorhouse E. of the road. At Herrings Green is a Queen Anne farmhouse.

EATON BRAY (9720), on flat land, has few damson orchards remaining. The manor of Eaton was granted by King John to William de Cantlowe in 1205; there are traces, including the moat, of the castle he built in 1221. Sir Reginald Bray, from whom the growing village takes its name, acquired the manor in 1490. He was treasurer and involved in the building of Henry VII's Chapel in Westminster Abbey.

The church, unremarkable Perp. outside, has very beautiful E.Eng. arcades – the superb N. arcade of cathedral quality in miniature. The magnificent wrought-iron scrolls of the S. door hinges are mid-13C. Two fire-hooks hang on the W. wall inside.

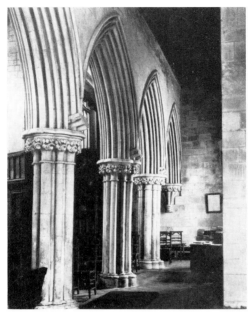

EATON BRAY: N. arcade c.1235

EATON SOCON (1759), in Huntingdonshire from 1965 and Cambridgeshire from 1974 (see **STAPLOE**).

EDWORTH (2241). This minute village was the scene of the Agnes Beaumont scandal involving John Bunyan. The Beaumont farmhouse stands near the Great North Road. It is related that in February 1467 Bunyan gave the fair Agnes a pillion ride to Gamlingay, to attend a meeting at which he was preaching. The tongue of scandal wagged happily, especially when Agnes's father died shortly afterwards. Bunyan was accused of giving her poison to administer to the old man, but an inquest absolved him. Agnes is buried at Hitchin, having married one Story. Some of her writings are in the British Museum.

Edworth was the home of a Roman, for a mosaic pavement was found under the old rectory. In fields the church, mostly Dec., has a mural, a rather rare Trans.-Norman pillar piscina in the N. aisle and carvings on the chancel stalls.

EGGINGTON (9525), a small village in the gault, is of little interest except for Eggington House, a Queen Anne house with late 18C attic storey. The church has been severely restored.

EGGINGTON House

ELSTOW (0547). Home of John Bunyan, site of an abbey and an attractive village, this is a place which the visitor to Bedfordshire never misses.

Bedford housing almost reaches it and unfortunately its High Street is the main road, but it keeps Tudor and Jacobean houses, and *The Swan*, all with timbers and overhangs, often (regrettably) pebble-rendered; also a few thatched cottages.

The Benedictine nunnery founded in the 11C by Judith, niece of the Conqueror, was one of the richest nunneries in England, the nuns drawn largely from landed families. It was surrendered to the king in 1539 and granted to Sir Humphrey Radcliffe fourteen years later. In 1616 it was purchased by Thomas Hillersdon, who built from part of the domestic buildings a lovely Renaissance mansion called Elstow Place, the ruins of which stand just S. of the church.

The church has a detached campanile like Marston Moretaine, its top Perp. on an earlier base. The church itself, the W. end of the cruciform abbey that extended some 115 feet farther E., has Perp. windows (perhaps re-used from parts demolished in 1580) in its E. wall. Inside, it is impressively lofty, with no division between nave and chancel. The three E. arches are massive early Norman work and the wider W. pair E.Eng., all scraped by Victorian restorers, who harshly reconstructed the Norman N. doorway with its finely-carved tympanum. A vaulted monastic room, used as a vestry, is probably 13C and has a unique vault-pattern. Details that have survived puritan iconoclasts and Victorian restorers include an excellent brass of 1427; also one to Abbess Elizabeth Hervey, 1527 – only one other brass to an abbess exists (at Denham, Bucks). A mural monument 1566 is to the Radcliffes who lived in the former nunnery, and two good tablets are to Hillersdons. The large Perp. font is the one at which Bunyan was baptised. The uncommon Perp. pulpit, with traceried panels, is now with Bunyan relics in the Moot Hall. New glass in E. windows of the aisles are Bunyan memorials.

ELSTOW: Moot Hall on the green

The early-Tudor Moot Hall on the green originally had six shops with a court or meeting room upstairs. Now, since restoration in 1951, a lower room is laid out with simple furniture of Bunyan's day – chest, cradle, table, chairs and bench on rush-matting. Upstairs is displayed more elaborate antique furniture of the same period; also there are early editions of Bunyan's many works. The other lower room has more intimate Bunyan relics – the pulpit, doors of his prison and various displays (see App. 4). Every May the green was the scene of a great fair, granted to the abbess by Henry II. It was still held in Bunyan's day and is said to have been the original of his *Vanity Fair*. Also on the green is the stump of the cross beneath which Bunyan was playing tipcat when he heard the 'Voice of Heaven'.

John Bunyan was born in 1628 near Harrowden (q.v.). His father was a tinker too and came from a family which has been traced back in this county for centuries, thus dispelling the theory that he was a gypsy. The young John, a child of dreams, haunted by strange fears of God and the Devil instilled by Puritan England, went to school at Bedford, though it seems doubtful that he received much education. For several years he practised the trade of tinker and was then pressed into the service of the Parliamentary army, at the age of seventeen. He was stationed for a time at Newport Pagnell and was probably at the siege of Leicester. He left the army in 1647 and, a year later, married a young woman as poor as he, 'not having so much household stuff as a dish or spoon between us'. This was the young bride he brought to Elstow. Today a plaque marks the site of their home at the N. end of the village. Here, in a forge he worked at tinkering and blind Mary, to whom he was devoted, was born in 1650.

We know something of the conflicts in his mind at this period, for he tells us of the awful doubts of conscience which came to him concerning his bell-ringing and dancing, two pastimes of which he was inordinately fond. The bell he rang still hangs in the campanile, which seemed to hold some terrible fascination for him. He read avidly of the Bible and such few other books as came his way until, in 1656, his call came and he began to hold religious meetings in the surrounding villages. So he continued for the next four years – preaching, writing, spreading the gospel as he saw it among the simple half-bewildered villagers of Commonwealth England.

Then, with the Restoration, came persecution. He was arrested near Harlington (q.v.) in 1660 and began his long term of imprisonment in Bedford county gaol. He enjoyed brief spells of freedom, lived then in Bedford and officiated at Congregational meetings. It is very doubtful if he ever saw the inside of the town gaol on old Bedford bridge, where he is popularly supposed to have been incarcerated.

He left prison twelve years later, only to return in 1675 for his obdurate refusal to 'toe the line'; it was during this second imprisonment that he began to write *The Pilgrim's Progress*. Altogether he wrote over